Kids to the Rescue!

First Aid Techniques for Kids

Written by Maribeth & Darwin Boelts
Illustrated by Marina Megale

The authors would like to thank the Boy Scouts of America, Irving, Texas; the American Heart Association, Dallas, Texas; and Sara Van Brocklin—a ten-year-old reader and friend.

The publisher would like to thank Dr. Jeffrey Lindenbaum of Group Health, Seattle, Wash.; Ron Rutherford, Ph.D. of Lifetek, Inc., Kirkland, Wash.; and Dr. Paul Mendelman, University of Washington School of Medicine, Dept. of Pediatrics, Seattle, Wash.—for their review of the text and first aid procedures. Special thanks also go to Stacey Shiovitz for a youthful review of the text and illustrations.

The illustrator thanks all those who helped model for the drawings: Rosanne and Suzanne Ritch; Matthew, Grant, and Virginia Kolkoske; Jesse and Nicky Wilke; and Sue and Shaunte Marie Gagner. Thanks, also to Selene the Snake for photo reference.

Published by
Parenting Press, Inc.
P.O. Box 75267
Seattle, WA 98125

Table of Contents

Note to Parents and Teachers

Children are natural learners. They are explorers, question-askers, and role-players. They learn by doing.

Kids to the Rescue meets children where they are and encourages:

- **Listening** to the first aid situation as it is read by an adult.
- **Looking** at the illustration and picturing themselves in the situation.
- **Telling** the adult what they would do in that scenario.
- **Role playing** the steps on the first aid page enough times so that recall is automatic.

The book is designed to utilize the adult as a child's helper. You can read the situation to a pre-reading child, or listen as the older child reads the text himself, and then help the children role play the first aid steps. It is important to say "Yes!" when children ask if they can run cold water on a "burn", or elevate a "swollen ankle." This pretending and role playing will help them remember.

You will see children grow in confidence as the first aid steps are mastered. It is empowering, not scary, to know that bleeding can be stopped with direct pressure, and that insect stings can be soothed with cold water.

Remember that children need to know emergency numbers and when they should use them. Practice dialing the numbers on a toy telephone, or on a real telephone with the receiver hook pressed down.

Accidents are the leading cause of death for children ages 1-14. Other children are most often present when an injury occurs. Knowing what to do right at the moment of injury can dramatically improve a child's chances for recovery.

Now, turn to that first situation and get ready to help a child help herself.

Kid's Introduction

All kids play together. Sometimes when you're playing with your friends, one of them gets hurt. Sometimes no grownups are around to help. Do you know what to do if your friend gets hurt? Do you know how to help yourself if *you* get hurt?

This book will show you how to help yourself and others. You can learn how to give first aid and get help.

Nose Bleed

You get a new aluminum bat and a real baseball for your birthday.

"Will you pitch some balls to me?" you ask your big brother.

"Sure, as long as you pitch some to me too," he says.

You walk to the playground by your apartment building. Your brother throws you the first ball. You hit a pop fly right to him.

"Good try," he says. "Try to keep it out of the air, though."

He pitches again. This time you hit a ground ball that rolls to the fence.

"That's better. You'd make it to second base on that one," he says. "Last pitch and then it's my turn to bat."

He winds up to pitch and then releases the ball. Your brother's aim is a little off and the ball hits you right on the nose! You touch your nose. Sure enough, it's bleeding.

How to help with a nose bleed:

■ **Squeeze your nose.** Take hold of the whole soft part of your nose and pinch it together.

■ **Look down.** As you pinch your nose, look down. Don't tip your head back.

■ **Squeeze for ten minutes.** Keep squeezing your nose for ten minutes before you let go.

■ **Check to see if your nose is still bleeding.** If it is, squeeze your nose some more. Check again. If the bleeding hasn't stopped, go get help.

☞ Hint: Squeeze the whole soft part of your nose and look down.

Something in the Eye

Your front yard is covered with a thick blanket of orange, red, and yellow leaves.

"Today would be a good day to rake," your dad says. "Would you like to do the front or back yard?"

"I'll do the back," you answer, even though you don't feel like raking very much.

As you work, large gray clouds begin to appear in the sky. The air feels funny, like it might rain. A strong gust of wind suddenly blows your pile of leaves up into the air. The wind stirs up the dirt and dust in the yard. You blink, but some of it gets into your eye.

How to help with something in the eye:

■ **Leave your eye alone.**
Do not rub or touch your eyeball. The dirt could scratch your eye and make it hurt worse.

■ **Use your eyelid to help.** Gently take hold of your upper eyelid and pull it carefully over the bottom eyelid. Then, still holding your eyelid, blink.

■ **Rinse your eye.** If using your eyelid didn't help, use water to rinse your eye. Hold your eye under a faucet or hose and rinse it with cold water. Be careful that the water doesn't run into your other eye.

■ **Go for help.** If your eye still doesn't feel better, go ask someone for help.

 Hint: Do not rub your eye.

Bleeding

Your cousin from Florida is visiting you for the week.

"It's warmer in Florida than it is in Maine," she says, shivering. "And your beaches are rockier."

"We can go back to my house to get your jacket and shoes," you offer.

"No, I'm okay. I want to look for shells. I want some really neat ones to take back with me to Florida," she answers. She runs up ahead to check out what looks like a beautiful, shiny shell. Suddenly, she stops and grabs her foot. "Ow! What did I step on?" she exclaims.

You catch up with her and see blood flowing from her heel. It's making a small pool in the sand. And in that puddle is a broken piece from a glass bottle.

How to help with bleeding:

- **Show your cousin how to press on the cut.** Tell her to press until the bleeding stops. If she has a clean scarf or a tissue, she can put that on the cut before she starts to push on it.

- **Elevate the cut.** Tell your cousin to sit down. You can raise her foot by putting something under it. You could roll your jacket up or use a backpack to put underneath her cut foot.

- **Go for help.** Tell your cousin to keep pushing on the cut. Call or go find help for her.

 Hint: Press right on a cut and elevate it.

Broken Bones

"Come on, I'll race you to the bridge!" you shout to your friend. You are riding on the bike trail near your home. Your friend accepts the challenge and speeds ahead. The trees and flowers along the trail become a blur as you pump the pedals, but your friend is still winning!

As he turns to see how far back you are, his bike heads straight for a large rock alongside the trail. He hits the rock and is thrown off his bike. As you race over to help him, you notice that his arm is bent in a funny way. Your friend is crying because his arm hurts so much.

How to help with broken bones:

■ **Yell for help!**

■ **Keep the hurt arm still.**
Don't move it. The bone may be broken. Tell your friend to stay exactly where he fell, unless it's a dangerous place.

■ **Check for bleeding.** If your friend has a cut, remember how to help. Have him press on the cut until the bleeding stops.

☞ Hint: Call for help and don't move a bone that might
be broken.

Dog Bite

You wake up one morning and glance sleepily at the clock. "Only 15 minutes to get ready for school!" you exclaim as you hop out of bed.

After a quick bowl of cereal and a few minutes spent brushing your teeth, combing your hair, and getting dressed, you head out the door.

You decide to take a shortcut to school. Halfway through an empty lot you hear the low, throaty growl of a dog. You turn to face him and you notice that his teeth are bared and his tail isn't wagging. You haven't seen him on your way to school before. You forget that you aren't supposed to move suddenly in front of an angry dog and you start to run. The dog chases you and then bites you on the arm.

How to help with a dog bite:

- **Notice what kind of dog bit you.** Look at him carefully. How big is he? What color fur does he have? Does he have long or short fur? Have you seen the dog before? If so, where?

- **Check for bleeding.** If it is, press on it to stop the bleeding. Wash the bite. Hold it under cold water.

- **Call for help.** If your mom and dad are at home, go tell them about the dog bite. Describe the dog.

 Hint: Notice what the dog looks like, and find a
grownup right away.

Snake Bite

It's the last day of summer camp. You and your best friend want to do something fun during the free period in the afternoon.

"Do you want to climb on the rocks in back of the lodge?" she asks.

"Sure, that sounds great," you reply.

After you tell the camp counselor where you will be, you both climb to the top of the rocks. You talk about the letters you'll write each other when you get back home. The time passes quickly.

"I think the free period is over," your friend says. "We should start heading back." She climbs down the rocks. Suddenly, she cries out. "A snake just bit me!" she screams.

You stop just in time to see a snake slither by.

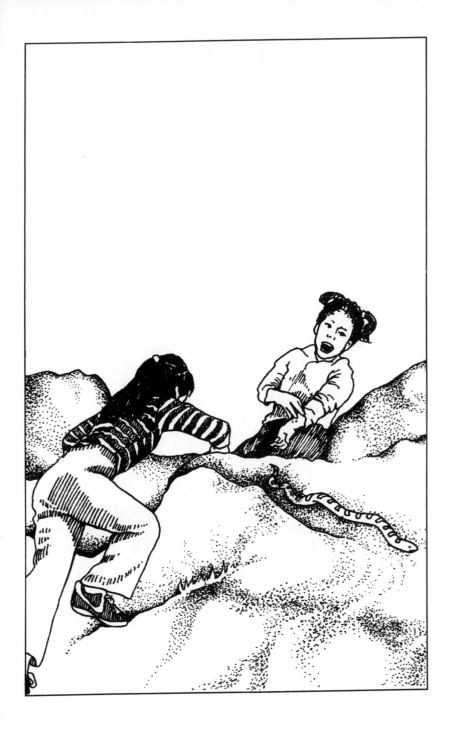

How to help with a snake bite:

■ **Lie down.** Your friend should lie down and try to stay very still. Keep the bite lower than her chest. This will keep the poison from reaching her heart too fast.

■ **Remember what the snake looks like and stay quiet.** A snake bite is a scary thing for both of you. You will help your friend by telling her that she will be okay. Say, "I'll find help. Don't move until I get back. It will be okay."

■ **Get help.** Yell for help, or go find help quickly. Tell a grownup what the snake looked like— what color it was and how big it was.

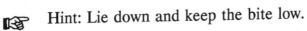 Hint: Lie down and keep the bite low.

Poisoning

You and your little brother are watching cartoons one Saturday morning. Your mother looks out the window and sees your neighbor struggling with a bag of groceries.

"I'm going out to help Mrs. Winters with her groceries. Will you please watch your brother for a few minutes?" she asks.

You nod your head and continue watching cartoons. You forget about keeping an eye on your little brother and he toddles off into the bathroom. A few minutes later he walks in front of the television. He says, "Yucky candy." You see an open pill bottle in his hand.

How to help with poisoning:

■ **Take the pill bottle away.**
Keep it away from your brother,
but close by. You will need to
know what kind of pills he ate
when you call the poison control
center.

■ **Call for help.** If you cannot
find your parents or another
grownup, dial the emergency
number. Then call the poison
control center to find out what to
do next.

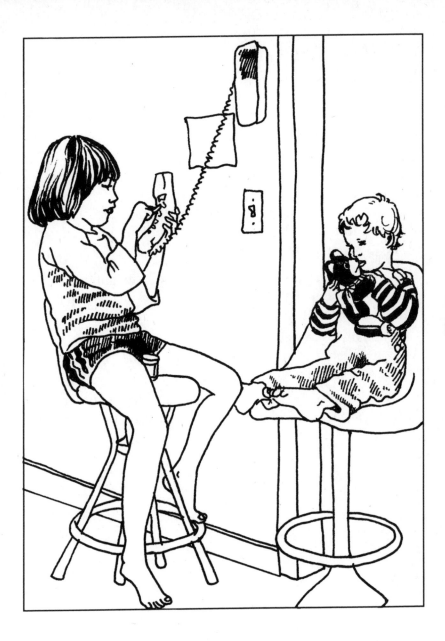

Hint: When someone eats or drinks something that *could be* poisonous, call the emergency number and the poison control center number.

Insect Sting

You and your father are busy loading the car for a camping trip. You don't notice when your new kitten Smokey darts out the front door. After everything is in the car, you can't find Smokey. You start looking around the house, but you can't find her. You decide to try looking outside.

"Smokey!" you call. "Smokey!"

As you cut across the driveway to your neighbor's flower garden, you hear a soft mewing. Bending low, you part the bushy flowers with your hands.

"Smokey?" you say. Two little green eyes peer out at you. As you reach for your kitten, a bee lands on your arm. Before you know it, the bee stings you.

"Ouch!" you cry, grabbing your arm with your other hand. Smokey is startled and quickly hides back under the bush.

How to help with an insect sting:

- **Shout for help.** If you are allergic to bee stings, get help quickly.

- **Put the bite under cold water.** Run the water on the insect sting until it feels a little better.

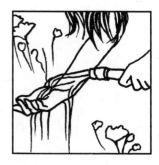

 Hint: Put the bite under cold water.

Chemical Burns in the Eye

It's moving day and everyone is busy. Your mom and dad run next door to the neighbors' to see if they have any extra boxes. You and your friend are supposed to pack up the few things left in the kitchen.

"Don't forget that stuff still on top of the refrigerator," your friend reminds you.

"That's just what I was going to do," you say. Standing on your tip toes, you reach for the top of the refrigerator. As you feel around for the items, you knock over a bottle of kitchen cleanser. The loose lid comes off and cleanser gets into your friend's eye.

How to help with chemicals in the eye:

■ **Run cool water on the eye.**
Quickly, lead your friend to a
sink. Tell him to lean over and
put his hurt eye under the cold
water from the faucet. Be
careful that the water doesn't run
into his other eye.

■ **Get help.** Call your parents
or another grownup while your
friend rinses his eye.

■ **Run cold water on his eye
for 15 minutes.** You can set a
timer to help you.

 Hint: Run cool water on the eye right away.

Choking

"Hey, your dad packed us a pretty good lunch," your friend says, as he unwraps three tuna fish sandwiches, a bunch of grapes, and a bag of cookies from the basket.

"We deserve it after the hiking we've done," your other friend tells him.

"How much further till we reach Pyramid Peak?" you ask.

"I think we're about halfway there. The sooner we finish lunch, the sooner we'll get there. Maybe we'll beat that group that's behind us," your friend says.

You quickly begin eating your lunch. One of your friends wolfs down his sandwich and pops a few grapes into his mouth. Suddenly, he grasps his throat. He can't talk or breathe. "Is he choking?" your other friend asks worriedly.

43

How to help with choking:

■ **Get behind your friend and position your hands.**
1. Place one hand on his shoulder and use the finger of your other hand to find his belly-button.
2. Place your fist above his belly button, then grab your fist with your other hand.

■ **Let your friend hang over your fists and thrust in, very hard, six to ten times.** If he still can't breathe, try again.

■ **Send for help.** Your other friend can find a grownup or call the emergency number. Tell him the emergency number:

_____.

44

☞ Hint: Place fist above belly button; grab fist with your other hand; thrust in very hard, six to ten times.

Electric Shock

Your mother has invited a friend and her two-year-old daughter over for lunch. After lunch, your mother asks you to play with the little girl up in your bedroom.

"Do you want to make a picture for your mom?" you ask. She smiles and nods her head.

"Okay. I'll cut and you can glue," you say.

There is an extra pair of scissors in your coloring box. While you are busy, the little girl takes the scissors and sticks them into the outlet on the wall. She screams and can't seem to let go of the scissors.

How to help with electric shock:

- **DON'T TOUCH HER!** Stay away from her. You, too, could get shocked if you touch her, and then you couldn't help her.

- **Get help right away.** Ask a grownup to push her away from the outlet with a wood chair or broom. A grownup can also shut off the electricity in the house.

☞ Hint: Never touch someone who is being shocked.
  Get help right away.

Burns

Your family shares a garden space with your neighbors.

"How about corn on the cob for supper tonight?" your mom asks.

"Great!" you answer. "Do you want me to go next door and pick some?"

"No, but I would like you to stay here in the house and let me know when this pot of water boils. I should have the corn picked by then," she says.

The pot of water simmers on the stove. Soon, there are little bubbles forming around the edges of the pot. You notice that the handle of the pot is facing the front of the stove. You decide to turn the handle toward the back of the stove. The pot tips as you turn it and some boiling hot water splashes onto your arm.

How to help with burns:

■ Put your hurt arm in cold water right away. Hold it under the faucet or put it in a pan of cold water. Keep your burn in cold water until it stops hurting.

■ Call a grownup. If the burn still hurts when it's out of the cold water, call your mother, or another grownup, to help.

Putting a burn in cold water helps, even if you got burned from fire, or something else that is hot.

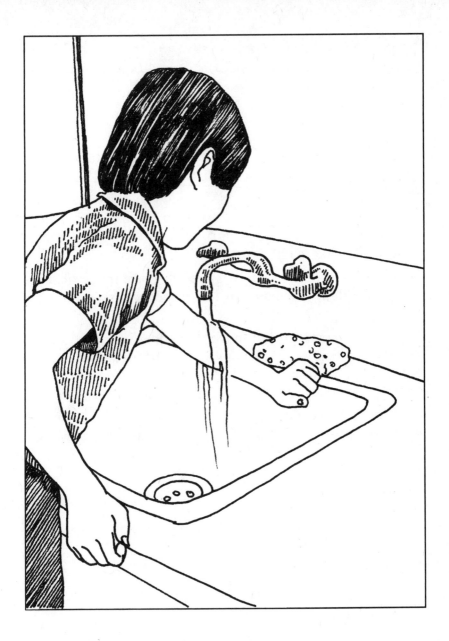

 Hint: Put a burn in cold water.

Unconsciousness

You are helping your aunt paint the living room in her new apartment.

"If you paint the low parts, I'll paint the high parts," she says. Then she climbs an old wooden ladder and begins to paint the ceiling. In just a short while the ceiling is covered with fresh, white paint.

"There," she says. "Do you see any place that I missed?" You see a dull, gray patch in the corner and point it out to her.

"No problem. I'll just move the ladder over and get that one spot," she says. As she quickly climbs back up the ladder and reaches up to paint, the ladder slips out from under her. She falls with a heavy thud to the ground.

You rush over to her. "Aunt Cathy!" you shout, but she does not answer or move. It is like she is asleep, but will not wake up. You wonder, is she unconscious?

How to help with unconsciousness:

■ **Don't touch her.** Do not try to move her.

■ **Call for help.** If a grownup is close by, ask for help.

■ **Dial the emergency number.** Say "My aunt fell and won't wake up." The dispatcher will ask you for your address and phone number, and tell you what to do next.

☞ Hint: Don't move an unconscious person. Call for
help right away.

Clothing on Fire

It is the last campout of the summer. The fire is blazing and the night sky is full of stars. You are roasting marshmallows with your family and talking about all the fun things you did over the summer.

As you talk, you notice that your sister's marshmallow is on fire.

"Here, I'll blow it out for you," you say and take it away from her. While you are helping her, your pant leg gets too close to the flames and catches on fire!

How to help with clothing on fire:

■ **STOP.** Freeze—don't move! Running will make the fire burn faster.

■ **DROP.** Lay down on the ground right away.

■ **ROLL.** Roll back and forth on the ground to put the fire out.

■ **Yell for help.** If people are close by, ask them for water to pour on your clothes.

    If your skin gets burned, remember how to take care of a burn. See page 52.

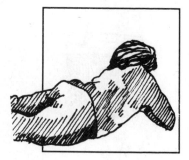

☞ Hint: If your clothing catches on fire, STOP, DROP, and ROLL.

Using the Phone to Get Help

EMERGENCY: 911

⬦ Address:
800 Main Street

☎ Phone:
631-1102

⚘ Neighbor's Phone:
631-8206

♀ Family Doctor:
Dr. Wilson
621-8356

⊗ Poison Control:
820-9151

You can practice calling the emergency number by pretending to call on a toy phone, or on a real, disconnected phone. A grownup can help you practice. Remember, we call the emergency number *only when we truly need help.*

If you are in a situation where someone is hurt and you can't find a grownup to help, dial the emergency number. Do not call the number unless you really need help.

After a grownup fills out the information on the emergency card (in the back of this book), hang it near your phone. It would be a good idea to practice dialing the number of your neighbor, family doctor, and the poison control center.

Using the phone, step by step:

■ **Dial the emergency number**

_____ .

■ **Tell the person on the line your name, address, and phone number.**
You can say—

"My **name** is

_____ .

My **address** is

_____ .

My **phone number** is _____ ."

■ **Tell the person why you need help.** The person who answers the phone will tell you when you can hang up.

 Hint: Give the dispatcher your name, address, and phone number, then say what is the matter.

Congratulations! You have just completed *Kids to the Rescue!* But wait a minute...do you think that you will remember all that you've learned? Do you know what will help you remember everything?

PRACTICE.

Keep this book in a place where you can find it easily. Use your little brother or sister, your best friend, or even your stuffed animal as a pretend patient. Talk through the first aid steps as you act them out. If you can't remember the steps, look at your book, or ask a grownup for help.

Use the quiz on the next pages to test yourself. Then keep practicing. You never know when you'll need to be a "kid to the rescue!"

First Aid Quiz

Try to choose the *best* answer to these first aid questions. If you are stumped, look for the answer in the book or in the key.

1. A good way to stop bleeding from a cut is to...

    A. Press next to the cut.
    B. Press on the cut.
    C. Run cold water on the cut.

2. If you burn yourself on a hot cookie sheet, you should...

    A. Press on it.
    B. Rub butter on the burn.
    C. Hold the burn under cold water until it feels better.

3. Your friend falls off a jungle gym. His leg looks funny. You should...

    A. Try to straighten the leg.
    B. Move him out from under the jungle gym.
    C. Shout for help. If no one comes, then go for help.

4. Someone is knocked unconscious. You should...

    A. Try to "wake her up."
    B. Move her to where she might be more comfortable.
    C. Call for help.

5. If you get something in your eye and you rub it, it could scratch the surface of your eye.

    A. True
    B. False

6. If your friend gets a chemical splashed in his eye, you should help him by having him rinse his eye for...

    A. 1 minute
    B. 15 minutes
    C. 5 minutes

7. When you are helping someone who is choking, where do you put your fists?

A. Just above his belly button.
B. Just below his belly button.
C. In your pockets.

8. Your nose starts to bleed while you are practicing cartwheels. You should...

A. Tilt your head back.
B. Ask your parents for an aspirin.
C. Pinch the whole soft part of your nose together and lean forward.

9. If you touch someone who is getting an electrical shock, you will get shocked too.

A. True
B. False

10. Cold water on an insect sting will help the hurting stop.

A. True
B. False

11. Your baby brother eats some poison by accident. The first thing you should do is...

A. Take away the poison.
B. Call for help.

12. If you are bitten by a dog, try to remember...

A. The size of the dog.
B. The color of the dog.
C. If you have seen the dog before.
D. All of the above.

13. Your clothes are on fire! You should...

A. Run and try to find water to put it out.
B. Stop, drop, and roll.
C. Try to take off the burning clothes.

Answer Key

Now check your answers below.

1. B. If you are bleeding, the quickest way to stop it is to press on the cut.

2. C. Cold water helps a burn.

3. C. Never try to move or straighten a hurt arm or leg. Shout or go for help.

4. C. You will need help right away if someone is unconscious.

5. A. True. Rubbing your eye when something is in it can scratch the surface of your eye.

6. B. You should have your friend rinse his eye for 15 minutes.

7. A. You place your fists just above the belly button.

8. C. If your nose starts to bleed, pinch the whole soft part together and lean forward.

9. A. True. *Never* touch a person who is getting an electrical shock. Call for help right away.

10. A. True. Cold water helps an insect sting feel better.

11. A. Take the poison away first and then call for help.

12. D. If you are bitten by a dog, try to remember as much about the dog as you can.

13. B. The best way to stop a fire is to stop, drop, and roll.

Alphabetical Index

EMERGENCY:

Address:

Phone:

Neighbor's Phone:

Family Doctor:

Poison Control:

More Books to Help Protect Children

It's MY Body, by Lory Freeman and illustrated by Carol Deach, teaches children how to distinguish between "good" and "bad" touches, and how to respond appropriately to unwanted touches. Useful with 3-8 years, 32 pages, $5.95 paper, $15.95 library

Mi Cuerpo Es MIO, Spanish translation of *It's MY Body.* $5.95 paper

Protect Your Child from Sexual Abuse by Janie Hart Rossi offers parents information about sexual abuse and what to do to prevent child abuse. Useful with 1-12 years, 64 pages, $7.95 paper, $17.95 library

Loving Touches, by Lory Freeman and illustrated by Carol Deach, teaches children how to ask for and give positive and nurturing touches. Children also learn how to respect their own and other's bodies. Useful with 3-8 years, 32 pages, $5.95 paper, $15.95 library

Telling Isn't Tattling, by Kathryn Hammerseng and illustrated by Dave Garbot, helps children learn when to tell an adult they need help, and when to deal with problems themselves. Adults learn when to pay attention to kids' requests for help. Useful with 4-12 years, 32 pages, $5.95 paper, $15.95 library

The Trouble with Secrets, by Karen Johnsen and illustrated by Linda Johnson Forssell, shows children how to distinguish between hurtful secrets and good surprises. Useful with 3-8 years, 32 pages, $5.95 paper, $15.95 library

Something Happened and I'm Scared to Tell, by Patricia Kehoe, Ph.D. and illustrated by Carol Deach, is the story of a young sexual abuse victim who learns how to recover self-esteem. Useful with 3-7 years, 32 pages, $5.95 paper, $15.95 library

Helping Abused Children by Patricia Kehoe, Ph.D. provides many ideas and activities for care givers working with sexually abused children. Useful with 3-12 years, 48 pages, $10.95 paper, $18.95 library

Something Is Wrong at My House, by Diane Davis and illustrated by Marina Megale, offers children in violent homes ways to cope with the violence. Useful with 3-12 years, 40 pages, $5.95 paper, $15.95 library

Kids to the Rescue!, by Maribeth and Darwin Boelts and illustrated by Marina Megale, uses an interactive "what-would-you-do-if?" format, and prompts kids to think wisely in an emergency. Useful with 4-12 years, 72 pages, $7.95 paper, $17.95 library

Ask for these books at your favorite bookstore, or call toll free 1-800-992-6657. VISA and MasterCard accepted with phone orders. Complete book catalog available on request.

Prices subject to change without notice.